M000026753

THE
SPIRIT-FILLED
POCKET BIBLE
ON
PROTECTION

Summit City Christian Center
2320 Maumee Ave
Fort Wayne, IN 46803
(219) 424-Love

THE
SPIRIT-FILLED
POCKET BIBLE
ON
PROTECTION

HARRISON HOUSE, INC.
Tulsa, Oklahoma

Unless otherwise indicated, all Scripture quotations are taken from the *King James Version* of the Bible.

The Spirit-Filled Pocket Bible on Protection
ISBN 0-89274-834-6
Copyright © 1995 by Harrison House, Inc.
P. O. Box 35035
Tulsa, Oklahoma 74153

Published by Harrison House, Inc.
P. O. Box 35035
Tulsa, Oklahoma 74153

The
Spirit-Filled
Pocket Bible
on Protection

Presented to

_____

By

_____

Date

_____

Introduction

One of the greatest keys to being covered with the protection of God — a covering that cannot be penetrated by the devil — is in the ability to hear the still small voice of the Spirit of God.

To be in tune with the Spirit of God and alert to His voice, you must know the covenant promises of God — the promises of His Word. God's Word and the still small voice of the Holy Spirit will always be in agreement.

As you appropriate God's promises of protection by believing, speaking, receiving and acting upon them, and as you follow the examples of protection in God's Word by angels, Jesus' shed blood, the name of Jesus, the Holy Spirit and the word of a true prophet (or prophetess), *nothing* will be able to stop you from walking out your God-ordained destiny! Absolutely nothing!

As you meditate in *The Spirit-Filled Pocket Bible on Protection*, may you be quickened to defy all natural restraints and forcibly head toward the "prize of the high calling of God in Christ Jesus" (Philippians 3:14).

Prayer

Father God, thank You for Your protection that is available to me through the promises of Your Word, the leading of the Holy Spirit, the shed blood of Jesus Christ, the name of Jesus and the armor You have provided.

Thank You, Lord, that in You I have a new bloodline and any holes in my armor of protection caused by generational curses or ancestral sins are plugged permanently, in Jesus' name.

Thank You, Father, for lifting up a standard against the enemy so my generation will mark a new beginning in accomplishing great exploits for Your Kingdom. We will seize Your Kingdom, Lord, by using the force of Your Word against the enemy.

Father, thank You for protecting me from the devil's calamities, tragedies, devastation and destruction, in Jesus' name.

Because I am empowered by Your Spirit, equipped with Your Word, Lord, and am willing and obedient to Your call upon my life, the enemy's tactics are dismantled in Jesus' all-powerful name before they hit the target of my life for which Satan has taken aim.

Thank You, Lord Jesus, for causing me to walk upon the high places of the earth. Amen.

After these things the word of the Lord came unto Abram in a vision, saying, Fear not, Abram: I am thy shield, and thy exceeding great reward.

Genesis 15:1

And the Lord appeared unto him [Isaac] the same night, and said, I am the God of Abraham thy father: fear not, for I am with thee, and will bless thee, and multiply thy seed for my servant Abraham's sake.

Genesis 26:24

And, behold, I am with thee [Jacob], and will keep thee in all places whither thou goest, and will bring thee again into this land; for I will not leave thee, until I have done that which I have spoken to thee of.

Genesis 28:15

And the Lord said unto Jacob, Return unto the land of thy fathers, and to thy kindred; and I will be with thee.

Genesis 31:3

And now do not be grieved or angry

with yourselves, because you sold me
here; for God sent me before you to preserve life.

And God sent me before you to preserve for you a remnant in the earth,
and to keep you alive by a great deliverance.

Genesis 45:5,7 NASB

And the Lord went before them by day
in a pillar of a cloud, to lead them the
way; and by night in a pillar of fire, to
give them light; to go by day and night:
He took not away the pillar of the
cloud by day, nor the pillar of fire by
night, from before the people.

Exodus 13:21,22

And Moses said to the people, "Do not
be afraid. Stand still, and see the salvation of the Lord, which He will accom-
plish for you today. For the Egyptians
whom you see today, you shall see again
no more for ever.

"The Lord will fight for you, and you
shall hold your peace."

Exodus 14:13,14 NKJV

Then the angel of God, who had been traveling in front of Israel's army, withdrew and went behind them. The pillar of cloud also moved from in front and stood behind them, coming between the armies of Egypt and Israel. Throughout the night the cloud brought darkness to the one side and light to the other side; so neither went near the other all night long.

Exodus 14:19,20 NIV

Then sang Moses and the children of Israel this song unto the Lord, and spake, saying, I will sing unto the Lord, for he hath triumphed gloriously: the horse and his rider hath he thrown into the sea.

The Lord is my strength and song, and he is become my salvation: he is my God, and I will prepare him an habitation; my father's God, and I will exalt him.

The Lord is a man of war: the Lord is his name.

Pharaoh's chariots and his host hath he cast into the sea: his chosen captains also are drowned in the Red sea.

The depths have covered them: they

13

sank into the bottom as a stone.

Thy right hand, O Lord, is become glorious in power: thy right hand, O Lord, hath dashed in pieces the enemy.

And in the greatness of thine excellency thou hast overthrown them that rose up against thee: thou sentest forth thy wrath, which consumed them as stubble.

And with the blast of thy nostrils the waters were gathered together, the floods stood upright as an heap, and the depths were congealed in the heart of the sea.

The enemy said, I will pursue, I will overtake, I will divide the spoil; my lust shall be satisfied upon them; I will draw my sword, my hand shall destroy them.

Thou didst blow with thy wind, the sea covered them: they sank as lead in the mighty waters.

Who is like unto thee, O Lord, among the gods? Who is like thee, glorious in holiness, fearful in praises, doing wonders?

Thou stretchedst out thy right hand, the earth swallowed them.

Thou in thy mercy hast led forth the people which thou hast redeemed: thou hast guided them in thy strength unto thy holy habitation.

Exodus 15:1-13

Behold, I send an Angel before thee, to keep thee in the way, and to bring thee into the place which I have prepared.

Exodus 23:20

I will send a panic in front of you, routing all the nations you reach, until your enemies all turn their backs in flight before you.

Exodus 23:27
Moffatt's Trans.

Therefore you shall do and give effect to My statutes and keep My ordinances and perform them, and you will dwell in the land in safety.

The land shall yield its fruit; you shall eat your fill and dwell there in safety.

Leviticus 25:18,19 AMP

If the Lord delight in us, then he will bring us into this land, and give it us; a land which floweth with milk and honey.

Only rebel not ye against the Lord, neither fear ye the people of the land; for they are bread for us: their defence is departed from them, and the Lord is with us: fear them not.

Numbers 14:8,9

Do not be shocked, nor fear them.

The Lord your God who goes before you will Himself fight on your behalf, just as He did for you in Egypt before your eyes,

And in the wilderness where you saw how the Lord your God carried you, just as a man carries his son, in all the way which you have walked, until you came to this place.

Deuteronomy 1:29-31 NASB

Ye shall not fear them; for the Lord your God he shall fight for you.

Deuteronomy 3:22

And the Lord commanded us to do all these statutes, to [reverently] fear the Lord our God for our good always, that He might preserve us alive, as it is this day.

And it will be accounted as righteousness (conformity to God's will in word, thought, and action) for us if we are watchful to do all this commandment before the Lord our God, as He has commanded us.

Deuteronomy 6:24,25 AMP

When you go to war against your enemies and see horses and chariots and an army greater than yours, do not be afraid of them, because the Lord your God, who brought you up out of Egypt, will be with you.

When you are about to go into battle, the priest shall come forward and address the army.

He shall say: "Hear, O Israel, today you are going into battle against your enemies. Do not be fainthearted or afraid; do not be terrified or give way to panic before them.

For the Lord your God is the one who goes with you to fight for you against your enemies to give you victory."

Deuteronomy 20:1-4 NIV

And it shall come to pass, if thou shalt hearken diligently unto the voice of the Lord thy God, to observe and to do all his commandments which I command thee this day, that the Lord thy God will set thee on high above all nations of the earth:

And all these blessings shall come on thee, and overtake thee, if thou shalt hearken unto the voice of the Lord thy God...

The Lord shall cause thine enemies that rise up against thee to be smitten before thy face: they shall come out against thee one way, and flee before thee seven ways...

The Lord shall establish thee an holy people unto himself, as he hath sworn unto thee, if thou shalt keep the commandments of the Lord thy God, and walk in his ways.

Deuteronomy 28:1,2,7,9

Be strong and of a good courage, fear not, nor be afraid of them: for the Lord thy God, he it is that doth go with thee; he will not fail thee, nor forsake thee.

Deuteronomy 31:6

For the Lord's portion is his people;
Jacob is the lot of his inheritance.

He found him in a desert land, and
in the waste howling wilderness; he led
him about, he instructed him, he kept
him as the apple of his eye.

As an eagle stirreth up her nest, flut-
tereth over her young, spreadeth abroad
her wings, taketh them, beareth them on
her wings:
So the Lord alone did lead him.

Deuteronomy 32:9-12a

About Benjamin he said: "Let the
beloved of the Lord rest secure in him,
for he shields him all day long, and the
one the Lord loves rests between his
shoulders."

Deuteronomy 33:12 NIV

The eternal God is thy refuge, and
underneath are the everlasting arms:
and he shall thrust out the enemy from
before thee; and shall say, Destroy them.

Israel then shall dwell in safety alone:
the fountain of Jacob shall be upon a
land of corn and wine; also his heavens
shall drop down dew.

Happy art thou, O Israel: who is like unto thee, O people saved by the Lord, the shield of thy help, and who is the sword of thy excellency! And thine enemies shall be found liars unto thee; and thou shalt tread upon their high places.

Deuteronomy 33:27-29

After the death of Moses the servant of the Lord, the Lord said to Joshua son of Nun, Moses' aide: "Moses my servant is dead. Now then, you and all these people, get ready to cross the Jordan River into the land I am about to give to them — to the Israelites. I will give you every place where you set your foot, as I promised Moses. Your territory will extend from the desert to Lebanon, and from the great river, the Euphrates — all the Hittite country — to the Great Sea on the west. No one will be able to stand up against you all the days of your life. As I was with Moses, so I will be with you; I will never leave you nor forsake you.

"Be strong and courageous, because you will lead these people to inherit the land I swore to their forefathers to give them. Be strong and very courageous. Be careful to obey all the law my servant Moses gave you; do not turn from it to the right or to the left, that you may be successful wherever you go. Do not let this Book of the Law depart from your mouth; meditate on it day and night, so that you may be careful to do everything written in it. Then you will be prosperous and successful.

Joshua 1:1-8 NIV

For the Lord our God, he it is that brought us up and our fathers out of the land of Egypt, from the house of bondage, and which did those great signs in our sight, and preserved us in all the way wherein we went, and among all the people through whom we passed:

And the Lord drave out from before us all the people, even the Amorites which dwelt in the land: therefore will we also serve the Lord; for he is our God.

Joshua 24:17,18

Stay with me, do not be afraid, for he

who seeks my life seeks your life; for you are safe with me.

1 Samuel 22:23 NASB

And he said, The Lord is my rock, and my fortress, and my deliverer;

The God of my rock; in him will I trust: he is my shield, and the horn of my salvation, my high tower, and my refuge, my saviour; thou savest me from violence.

I will call on the Lord, who is worthy to be praised: so shall I be saved from mine enemies.

2 Samuel 22:2-4

In my distress I called upon the Lord, and cried to my God: and he did hear my voice out of his temple, and my cry did enter into his ears.

2 Samuel 22:7

For thou art my lamp, O Lord: and the Lord will lighten my darkness.

For by thee I have run through a troop: by my God have I leaped over a wall.

As for God, his way is perfect; the

word of the Lord is tried: he is a buckler to all them that trust in him.

For who is God, save the Lord? and who is a rock, save our God?

God is my strength and power: and he maketh my way perfect.

He maketh my feet like hinds' feet: and setteth me upon my high places.

He teacheth my hands to war; so that a bow of steel is broken by mine arms.

Thou hast also given me the shield of thy salvation: and thy gentleness hath made me great.

Thou hast enlarged my steps under me; so that my feet did not slip.

2 Samuel 22:29-37

For you have given me strength for the battle and have caused me to subdue all those who rose against me.

You have made my enemies turn and run away; I have destroyed them all.

2 Samuel 22:40,41 TLB

Blessed be God who destroys those who oppose me and rescues me from my enemies. Yes, you hold me safe above their heads. You deliver me from violence.

No wonder I give thanks to you, O Lord, among the nations, and sing praises to your name.

2 Samuel 22:48-50 TLB

But he [Elijah] himself went a day's journey into the wilderness, and came and sat down under a broom tree. And he prayed that he might die, and said, "It is enough! Now, Lord, take my life, for I am no better than my fathers!"

Then as he lay and slept under a broom tree, suddenly an angel touched him, and said to him, "Arise and eat."

Then he looked, and there by his head was a cake baked on coals, and a jar of water. So he ate and drank, and lay down again.

And the angel of the Lord came back the second time, and touched him, and said, "Arise and eat, because the journey is too great for you."

So he arose, and ate and drank; and he went in the strength of that food forty days and forty nights as far as Horeb, the mountain of God.

And there he went into a cave, and spent the night in that place; and behold, the word of the Lord came to him, and He said to him, "What are you doing here, Elijah?"

So he said, "I have been very zealous for the Lord God of hosts; for the children of Israel have forsaken Your covenant, torn down Your altars, and killed Your prophets with the sword. I alone am left; and they seek to take my life."

Then He said, "Go out, and stand on the mountain before the Lord." And behold, the Lord passed by, and a great and strong wind tore into the mountains and broke the rocks in pieces before the Lord, but the Lord was not in the wind; and after the wind an earthquake, but the Lord was not in the earthquake;

And after the earthquake a fire, but the Lord was not in the fire; and after the fire a still small voice.

So it was, when Elijah heard it, that he wrapped his face in his mantle and went out and stood in the entrance of the cave. Suddenly a voice came to him, and said, "What are you doing here, Elijah?"

And he said, "I have been very zealous for the Lord God of hosts; because the children of Israel have forsaken Your covenant, torn down Your altars, and killed Your prophets with the sword. I alone am left; and they seek to take my life."

Then the Lord said to him: "Go, return on your way to the Wilderness of Damascus; and when you arrive, anoint Hazael as king over Syria.

"Also you shall anoint Jehu the son of Nimshi as king over Israel. And Elisha the son of Shaphat of Abel Meholah you shall anoint as prophet in your place.

"It shall be that whoever escapes the sword of Hazael, Jehu will kill; and whoever escapes the sword of Jehu, Elisha will kill.

"Yet I have reserved seven thousand in Israel, all whose knees have not bowed to Baal."

1 Kings 19:4-18a NKJV

Fear not: for they that be with us are more than they that be with them.

2 Kings 6:16

Jabez cried out to the God of Israel, "Oh, that you would bless me and enlarge my territory! Let your hand be with me, and keep me from harm so that I will be free from pain." And God granted his request.

1 Chronicles 4:10 NIV

Therefore David enquired again of God; and God said unto him, Go not up after them; turn away from them, and come upon them over against the mulberry trees.

And it shall be, when thou shalt hear a sound of going in the tops of the mulberry trees, that then thou shalt go out to battle: for God is gone forth before thee to smite the host of the Philistines.

David therefore did as God commanded him: and they smote the host of the Philistines from Gibeon even to Gazer.

And the fame of David went out into all the lands; and the Lord brought the fear of him upon all nations.

1 Chronicles 14:14-17

Be strong and courageous, be not afraid nor dismayed for the king of Assyria, nor for all the multitude that is with him: for there be more with us than with him:

27

With him is an arm of flesh; but with us is the Lord our God to help us, and to fight our battles. And the people rested themselves upon the words of Hezekiah king of Judah.

2 Chronicles 32:7,8

On the twelfth day of the first month we set out from the Ahava Canal to go to Jerusalem. The hand of our God was on us, and he protected us from enemies and bandits along the way.

Ezra 8:31 NIV

So the wall was completed on the twenty-fifth of Elul, in fifty-two days. When all our enemies heard about this, all the surrounding nations were afraid and lost their self-confidence, because they realized that this work had been done with the help of our God.

Nehemiah 6:15,16 NIV

You can have hope and feel secure, you can look round you and lie down in safety, lie down with no one to alarm you.

Job 11:18,19a
Moffatt's Trans.

Lord, how are they increased that trouble me! Many are they that rise up against me.

Many there be which say of my soul, There is no help for him in God. Selah.

But thou, O Lord, art a shield for me; my glory, and the lifter up of mine head.

I cried unto the Lord with my voice, and he heard me out of his holy hill. Selah.

I laid me down and slept; I awaked; for the Lord sustained me.

I will not be afraid of ten thousands of people, that have set themselves against me round about.

Arise, O Lord; save me, O my God: for thou hast smitten all mine enemies upon the cheek bone; thou hast broken the teeth of the ungodly.

Psalm 3:1-7

I will both lie down in peace, and sleep; for You alone, O Lord, make me dwell in safety.

Psalm 4:8 NKJV

Lead me, O Lord, in thy righteousness
because of mine enemies; make thy way
straight before my face.

Psalm 5:8

But let all those that put their trust in
thee rejoice: let them ever shout for joy,
because thou defendest them: let them
also that love thy name be joyful in thee.

For thou, Lord, wilt bless the righteous; with favour wilt thou compass
him as with a shield.

Psalm 5:11,12

5
O Lord my God, in thee do I put my
trust: save me from all them that persecute me, and deliver me.

Psalm 7:1

O righteous God, who searches minds
and hearts, bring to an end the violence
of the wicked and make the righteous
secure.

My shield is God Most High, who
saves the upright in heart.

Psalm 7:9,10 NIV

The Lord also will be a refuge for the oppressed, a refuge in times of trouble.

Psalm 9:9

The Lord replies, "I will arise and defend the oppressed, the poor, the needy. I will rescue them as they have longed for me to do."

The Lord's promise is sure. He speaks no careless word; all he says is purest truth, like silver seven times refined.

O Lord, we know that you will forever preserve your own from the reach of evil men.

Psalm 12:5-7 TLB

Preserve me, O God: for in thee do I put my trust.

Psalm 16:1

Concerning the works of men, by the word of thy lips I have kept me from the paths of the destroyer.

Hold up my goings in thy paths, that my footsteps slip not.

I have called upon thee, for thou wilt hear me, O God: incline thine ear unto me, and hear my speech.

Shew thy marvellous loving kindness, O thou that savest by thy right hand them which put their trust in thee from those that rise up against them.

Keep me as the apple of the eye, hide me under the shadow of thy wings.

Psalm 17:4-8

The Lord is my rock, and my fortress, and my deliverer; my God, my strength, in whom I will trust; my buckler, and the horn of my salvation, and my high tower.

I will call upon the Lord, who is worthy to be praised: so shall I be saved from mine enemies.

The sorrows of death compassed me, and the floods of ungodly men made me afraid.

The sorrows of hell compassed me about: the snares of death prevented me.

In my distress I called upon the Lord, and cried unto my God: he heard my voice out of his temple, and my cry came before him, even into his ears.

Psalm 18:2-6

He delivered me from my strong enemy, and from them which hated me: for they were too strong for me.

They prevented me in the day of my calamity: but the Lord was my stay.

He brought me forth also into a large place; he delivered me, because he delighted in me.

Psalm 18:17-19

For You will save the humble people, but will bring down haughty looks.

For You will light my lamp; the Lord my God will enlighten my darkness.

For by You I can run against a troop, by my God I can leap over a wall.

As for God, His way is perfect; the word of the Lord is proven; He is a shield to all who trust in Him.

For who is God, except the Lord? And who is a rock, except our God?

It is God who arms me with strength, and makes my way perfect.

He makes my feet like the feet of deer, and sets me on my high places.

He teaches my hands to make war, so that my arms can bend a bow of bronze.

You have also given me the shield of Your salvation; Your right hand has held me up, and Your gentleness has made me great.

You enlarged my path under me, so my feet did not slip.

Psalm 18:27-36 NKJV

The Lord lives! Blessed be my Rock! Let the God of my salvation be exalted.

It is God who avenges me, and subdues the peoples under me;

He delivers me from my enemies. You also lift me up above those who rise against me; You have delivered me from the violent man.

Psalm 18:46-48 NKJV

May the Lord answer you in the day of trouble! May the name of the God of Jacob set you up on high [and defend you];

Send you help from the sanctuary and support, refresh, and strengthen you from Zion.

Psalm 20:1,2 AMP

Now I know that the Lord saves His anointed; He will answer him from His holy heaven with the saving strength of

His right hand.

Some trust in chariots, and some in horses; but we will remember the name of the Lord our God.

They have bowed down and fallen; but we have risen and stand upright.

Save, Lord! May the King answer us when we call.

Psalm 20:6-9 NKJV

For the king trusteth in the Lord, and through the mercy of the most High he shall not be moved.

Psalm 21:7

For the king's trust is in the Eternal, and by the goodness of the Most High he stands unmoved.

Psalm 21:7
Moffatt's Trans.

But be not thou far from me, O Lord: O my strength, haste thee to help me...

Ye that fear the Lord, praise him; all ye the seed of Jacob, glorify him; and fear him, all ye the seed of Israel.

For he hath not despised nor abhorred the affliction of the afflicted; neither hath he hid his face from him; but when he cried unto him, he heard.

Psalm 22:19,23,24

The Lord is my shepherd, I shall not be in want.

He makes me lie down in green pastures, he leads me beside quiet waters, he restores my soul. He guides me in paths of righteousness for his name's sake.

Even though I walk through the valley of the shadow of death, I will fear no evil, for you are with me; your rod and your staff, they comfort me.

You prepare a table before me in the presence of my enemies. You anoint my head with oil; my cup overflows.

Surely goodness and love will follow me all the days of my life, and I will dwell in the house of the Lord forever.

Psalm 23:1-6 NIV

Lift up your heads, O you gates; and be lifted up, you age-abiding doors, that the King of glory may come in.

Who is the King of glory? The Lord strong and mighty, the Lord mighty in battle.

Lift up your heads, O you gates; yes, lift them up, you age-abiding doors, that the King of glory may come in.

Who is [He then] this King of glory? The Lord of hosts, He is the King of glory. Selah [pause, and think of that]!

Psalm 24:7-10 AMP

O my God, I trust in thee: let me not be ashamed, let not mine enemies triumph over me.

Yea, let none that wait on thee be ashamed: let them be ashamed which transgress without cause.

Shew me thy ways, O Lord; teach me thy paths.

Lead me in thy truth, and teach me: for thou art the God of my salvation; on thee do I wait all the day.

Psalm 25:2-5

The meek will he guide in judgment: and the meek will he teach his way.

All the paths of the Lord are mercy and truth unto such as keep his covenant and his testimonies.

Psalm 25:9,10

Asign me Godliness and Integrity as my bodyguards, for I expect you to protect me and to ransom Israel from all her troubles.

Psalm 25:21,22 TLB

The Lord is my strength and my shield; my heart trusted in him, and I am helped: therefore my heart greatly rejoiceth; and with my song will I praise him.

The Lord is their strength, and he is the saving strength of his anointed.

Save thy people, and bless thine inheritance: feed them also, and lift them up for ever.

Psalm 28:7-9

Turn your ear to me, come quickly to my rescue; be my rock of refuge, a strong fortress to save me.

Since you are my rock and my fortress, for the sake of your name lead and guide me.

Free me from the trap that is set for

me, for you are my refuge.

Into your hands I commit my spirit; redeem me, O Lord, the God of truth.

I hate those who cling to worthless idols; I trust in the Lord.

I will be glad and rejoice in your love, for you saw my affliction and knew the anguish of my soul.

You have not handed me over to the enemy but have set my feet in a spacious place.

Psalm 31:2-8 NIV

But I trust in you, O Lord; I say, "You are my God."

My times are in your hands; deliver me from my enemies and from those who pursue me.

Let your face shine on your servant; save me in your unfailing love.

Let me not be put to shame, O Lord, for I have cried out to you; but let the wicked be put to shame....

Psalm 31:14-17 NIV

How great is your goodness, which you have stored up for those who fear you, which you bestow in the sight of men on those who take refuge in you.

In the shelter of your presence you hide them from the intrigues of men; in your dwelling you keep them safe from accusing tongues.

Psalm 31:19,20 NIV

Love the Lord, all his saints! The Lord preserves the faithful, but the proud he pays back in full.

Be strong and take heart, all you who hope in the Lord.

Psalm 31:23,24 NIV

Thou art my hiding place; thou shalt preserve me from trouble; thou shalt compass me about with songs of deliverance. Selah.

I will instruct thee and teach thee in the way which thou shalt go: I will guide thee with mine eye.

Psalm 32:7,8

The Eternal wrecks the purposes of pagans, he brings to nothing what the nations plan.

Psalm 33:10
Moffatt's Trans.

Our inner selves wait [earnestly] for the Lord; He is our Help and our Shield.

For in Him does our heart rejoice, because we have trusted (relied on and been confident) in His holy name.

Psalm 33:20,21 AMP

This poor man cried, and the Lord heard him, and saved him out of all his troubles.

The angel of the Lord encampeth round about them that fear him, and delivereth them.

Psalm 34:6,7

The eyes of the Lord are upon the righteous, and his ears are open unto their cry.

The face of the Lord is against them that do evil, to cut off the remembrance of them from the earth.

The righteous cry, and the Lord heareth, and delivereth them out of all their troubles.

The Lord is nigh unto them that are of a broken heart; and saveth such as be of a contrite spirit.

41

Many are the afflictions of the righteous: but the Lord delivereth him out of them all.

He keepeth all his bones: not one of them is broken.

Evil shall slay the wicked: and they that hate the righteous shall be desolate.

The Lord redeemeth the soul of his servants: and none of them that trust in him shall be desolate.

Psalm 34:15-22

Plead my cause, O Lord, with them that strive with me: fight against them that fight against me.

Take hold of shield and buckler, and stand up for mine help.

Draw out also the spear, and stop the way against them that persecute me: say unto my soul, I am thy salvation.

Let them be confounded and put to shame that seek after my soul: let them be turned back and brought to confusion that devise my hurt.

Psalm 35:1-4

Trust in the Lord, and do good; so shalt

thou dwell in the land, and verily thou shalt be fed.

Delight thyself also in the Lord; and he shall give thee the desires of thine heart.

Commit thy way unto the Lord; trust also in him; and he shall bring it to pass.

And he shall bring forth thy righteousness as the light, and thy judgment as the noonday.

Rest in the Lord, and wait patiently for him: fret not thyself because of him who prospereth in his way, because of the man who bringeth wicked devices to pass.

Cease from anger, and forsake wrath: fret not thyself in any wise to do evil.

For evildoers shall be cut off: but those that wait upon the Lord, they shall inherit the earth.

For yet a little while, and the wicked shall not be: yea, thou shalt diligently consider his place, and it shall not be.

But the meek shall inherit the earth; and shall delight themselves in the abundance of peace.

Psalm 37:3-11

The steps of a good man are ordered by

the Lord, and He delights in his way.

Though he fall, he shall not be utterly cast down; for the Lord upholds him with His hand.

Psalm 37:23,24 NKJV

For the Lord loves justice, and does not forsake His saints; they are preserved forever, but the descendants of the wicked shall be cut off.

Psalm 37:28 NKJV

But the salvation of the righteous is of the Lord: he is their strength in the time of trouble.

And the Lord shall help them, and deliver them: he shall deliver them from the wicked, and save them, because they trust in him.

Psalm 37:39,40

I waited patiently for the Lord; and he inclined unto me, and heard my cry.

He brought me up also out of an horible pit, out of the miry clay, and set my feet upon a rock, and established my goings.

Psalm 40:1,2

Withhold not thou thy tender mercies from me, O Lord: let thy lovingkindness and thy truth continually preserve me.

Psalm 40:11

Let all who seek Thee rejoice and be glad in Thee; let those who love Thy salvation say continually, "The Lord be magnified!"

Since I am afflicted and needy, let the Lord be mindful of me; Thou art my help and my deliverer; do not delay, O my God.

Psalm 40:16,17 NASB

Blessed is he that considereth the poor: the Lord will deliver him in time of trouble.

The Lord will preserve him, and keep him alive; and he shall be blessed upon the earth: and thou wilt not deliver him unto the will of his enemies.

Psalm 41:1,2

By this I know that thou favourest me, because mine enemy doth not triumph over me.

And as for me, thou upholdest me in

mine integrity, and settest me before thy
face for ever.

Psalm 41:11,12

Through thee will we push down our
enemies: through thy name will we tread
them under that rise up against us.

For I will not trust in my bow, neither shall my sword save me.

But thou hast saved us from our enemies, and hast put them to shame that
hated us.

Psalm 44:5-7

God is our refuge and strength, a very
present help in trouble.

Therefore will not we fear, though
the earth be removed, and though the
mountains be carried into the midst of
the sea;

Though the waters thereof roar and
be troubled, though the mountains
shake with the swelling thereof. Selah.

There is a river, the streams whereof
shall make glad the city of God, the holy
place of the tabernacles of the most
High.

God is in the midst of her; she shall

not be moved: God shall help her, and
that right early.

Psalm 46:1-5

The Lord of hosts is with us; the God of
Jacob is our refuge. Selah.

Come, behold the works of the Lord,
what desolations he hath made in the
earth.

He maketh wars to cease unto the
end of the earth; he breaketh the bow,
and cutteth the spear in sunder; he bur-
neth the chariot in the fire.

Be still, and know that I am God: I
will be exalted among the heathen, I will
be exalted in the earth.

The Lord of hosts is with us; the God
of Jacob is our refuge. Selah.

Psalm 46:7-11

Great is the Eternal, loudly to be praised
within the city of our God, upon his
sacred hill.

High and fair on the northern slope,
the joy of all the world, the hill of Sion
lies, the city of the great King.

Within her citadels has God shown
himself her defense.

For yonder kings combined, invaded her;

But scared with panic at her sight, they took to flight,

Seized with a shudder, like women in the pangs of labour,

Shattered like merchantmen wrecked by an east wind.

What once we heard of, now our eyes have seen within the city of the Lord of hosts; God does preserve it evermore, the city of our God.

And so within thy temple we are thinking of thy goodness, O God;

Thy fame shall echo, like thy name, to the very ends of the earth, for thy right hand is full of victories.

Let Sion hill rejoice, let the towns of Judah joy, over thy saving deeds.

Walk about Sion, go round her, count up her towers, review her ramparts, scan her citadels, that you may tell the age to come what a God our God is for evermore.

Psalm 48:1-14
Moffatt's Trans.

Call upon me in the day of trouble; I

will deliver you, and you will honor me.

Psalm 50:15 NIV

Behold, God is my helper and ally; the Lord is my upholder and is with them who uphold my life.

He will pay back evil to my enemies; in Your faithfulness [Lord] put an end to them.

With a freewill offering I will sacrifice to You; I will give thanks and praise Your name, O Lord, for it is good.

For He has delivered me out of every trouble, and my eye has looked [in triumph] on my enemies.

Psalm 54:4-7 AMP

As for me, I will call upon God, and the Lord shall save me.

Evening and morning and at noon I will pray, and cry aloud, and He shall hear my voice.

He has redeemed my soul in peace from the battle that was against me, for there were many against me.

Psalm 55:16-18 NKJV

49

Cast thy burden upon the Lord, and he shall sustain thee: he shall never suffer the righteous to be moved.

Psalm 55:22

What time I am afraid, I will trust in thee.

In God I will praise his word, in God I have put my trust; I will not fear what flesh can do unto me...

In God have I put my trust: I will not be afraid what man can do unto me.

Psalm 56:3,4,11

For thou hast delivered my soul from death: wilt not thou deliver my feet from falling, that I may walk before God in the light of the living?

Psalm 56:13

My heart is fixed, O God, my heart is fixed: I will sing and give praise.

Psalm 57:7

Deliver me from mine enemies, O my God: defend me from them that rise up against me.

Psalm 59:1

I will wait for You, O You his Strength;
for God is my defense.

My God of mercy shall come to meet
me; God shall let me see my desire on
my enemies.

Psalm 59:9,10 NKJV

But I will sing of Your power; yes, I will
sing aloud of Your mercy in the morning; for You have been my defense and
refuge in the day of my trouble.

To You, O my Strength, I will sing
praises; for God is my defense, my God
of mercy.

Psalm 59:16,17 NKJV

Truly my soul waiteth upon God: from
him cometh my salvation.

He only is my rock and my salvation;
he is my defence; I shall not be greatly
moved.

Psalm 62:1,2

My soul, wait thou only upon God; for my expectation is from him.

He only is my rock and my salvation: he is my defence; I shall not be moved.

In God is my salvation and my glory: the rock of my strength, and my refuge, is in God.

Trust in him at all times; ye people, pour out your heart before him: God is a refuge for us. Selah.

Psalm 62:5-8

Hear my voice, O God, in my complaint; guard and preserve my life from the terror of the enemy.

Hide me from the secret counsel and conspiracy of the ungodly, from the scheming of evildoers.

Psalm 64:1,2 AMP

Oh, bless our God, you peoples! And make the voice of His praise to be heard,

Who keeps our soul among the living, and does not allow our feet to be moved.

Psalm 66:8,9 NKJV

But as for me, my prayer is to You, O

Lord, in the acceptable time; O God, in the multitude of Your mercy, hear me in the truth of Your salvation.

Deliver me out of the mire, and let me not sink; let me be delivered from those who hate me, and out of the deep waters.

Let not the floodwater overflow me, nor let the deep swallow me up; and let not the pit shut its mouth on me.

Hear me, O Lord, for Your lovingkindness is good; turn to me according to the multitude of Your tender mercies.

And do not hide Your face from Your servant, for I am in trouble; hear me speedily.

Draw near to my soul, and redeem it; deliver me because of my enemies.

Psalm 69:13-18 NKJV

For he shall deliver the needy when he crieth; the poor also, and him that hath no helper.

He shall spare the poor and needy, and shall save the souls of the needy.

Psalm 72:12,13

Thou shalt guide me with thy counsel, and afterward receive me to glory.

Whom have I in heaven but thee? And there is none upon earth that I desire beside thee.

My flesh and my heart faileth: but God is the strength of my heart, and my portion for ever.

For, lo, they that are far from thee shall perish: thou hast destroyed all them that go a whoring from thee.

But it is good for me to draw near to God: I have put my trust in the Lord God, that I may declare all thy works.

Psalm 73:24-28

At thy rebuke, O God of Jacob, both the chariot and horse are cast into a dead sleep.

Psalm 76:6

O my people, hear my teaching; listen to the words of my mouth.

I will open my mouth in parables, I will utter hidden things, things from of old —

What we have heard and known, what our fathers have told us.

We will not hide them from their children; we will tell the next generation the praiseworthy deeds of the Lord, his power, and the wonders he has done.

He decreed statutes for Jacob and established the law in Israel, which he commanded our forefathers to teach their children,

So the next generation would know them, even the children yet to be born, and they in turn would tell their children.

Then they would put their trust in God and would not forget his deeds but would keep his commands.

Psalm 78:1-7 NIV

He guided them with the cloud by day and with light from the fire all night.

Psalm 78:14 NIV

Vindicate the weak and fatherless; do justice to the afflicted and destitute.

Rescue the weak and needy; deliver them out of the hand of the wicked.

Psalm 82:3,4 NASB

Behold, O God our shield, and look

upon the face of thine anointed.

For a day in thy courts is better than a thousand. I had rather be a doorkeeper in the house of my God, than to dwell in the tents of wickedness.

For the Lord God is a sun and shield: the Lord will give grace and glory: no good thing will he withhold from them that walk uprightly.

O Lord of hosts, blessed is the man that trusteth in thee.

Psalm 84:9-12

Show us Thy lovingkindness, O Lord, and grant us Thy salvation.

I will hear what God the Lord will say; for He will speak peace to His people, to His godly ones; but let them not turn back to folly.

Surely His salvation is near to those who fear Him, that glory may dwell in our land.

Psalm 85:7-9 NASB

For thou hast a great love to me, O Lord, saving me from the very depths of death.

Psalm 86:13
Moffatt's Trans.

O Lord God of hosts, who is a strong Lord like unto thee? Or to thy faithfulness round about thee?

Psalm 89:8

Thou hast a mighty arm: strong is thy hand, and high is thy right hand.

Justice and judgment are the habitation of thy throne: mercy and truth shall go before thy face.

Blessed is the people that know the joyful sound: they shall walk, O Lord, in the light of thy countenance.

In thy name shall they rejoice all the day: and in thy righteousness shall they be exalted.

For thou art the glory of their strength: and in thy favour our horn shall be exalted.

For the Lord is our defence; and the Holy One of Israel is our king.

Psalm 89:13-18

He who dwells in the shelter of the Most High will rest in the shadow of the Almighty.

I will say of the Lord, "He is my refuge and my fortress, my God, in whom I trust."

Surely he will save you from the fowler's snare and from the deadly pestilence.

He will cover you with his feathers, and under his wings you will find refuge; his faithfulness will be your shield and rampart.

You will not fear the terror of night, nor the arrow that flies by day,

Nor the pestilence that stalks in the darkness, nor the plague that destroys at midday.

A thousand may fall at your side, ten thousand at your right hand, but it will not come near you.

You will only observe with your eyes and see the punishment of the wicked.

If you make the Most High your dwelling — even the Lord, who is my refuge —

Then no harm will befall you, no disaster will come near your tent.

For he will command his angels concerning you to guard you in all your ways;

They will lift you up in their hands, so that you will not strike your foot against a stone.

You will tread upon the lion and the cobra; you will trample the great lion and the serpent.

"Because he loves me," says the Lord, "I will rescue him; I will protect him, for he acknowledges my name.

He will call upon me, and I will answer him; I will be with him in trouble, I will deliver him and honor him.

With long life will I satisfy him and show him my salvation."

Psalm 91:1-16 NIV

Happy the man who stays by the Most High in shelter, who lives under the shadow of Almighty God,

Who calls the Eternal "My refuge and my fortress, my God in whom I trust"!

He saves you from the fowler's snare and from the deadly pit;

He protects you with his pinions and hides you underneath his wings.

You need not fear the terrors of the night, nor arrows flying in the day;

You need not fear plague stalking in the dark, nor sudden death at noon;

Hundreds may fall beside you, thousands at your right hand, but the plague will never reach you,

Safe shielded by his faithfulness.

You have only to look on and see

how evil men are punished;

But you have sheltered beside the Eternal, and made the Most High God your home,

So no scathe can befall you, no plague can approach your tent.

For he puts you under his angels' charge, to guard you wherever you go,

To lift you in their hands lest you trip over a stone;

You can walk over reptiles and cobras, trampling on lions and on dragons.

"He clings to me, so I deliver him; I set him safe, because he cares for me;

I will answer his cry and be with him in trouble, delivering him and honouring him;

I will satisfy him with long life, and let him see my saving care."

Psalm 91:1-16
Moffatt's Trans.

Unless the Lord had given me help, I would soon have dwelt in the silence of death.

When I said, "My foot is slipping," your love, O Lord, supported me.

Psalm 94:17,18 NIV

But the Lord has become my fortress, and my God the rock in whom I take refuge.

Psalm 94:22 NIV

O come, let us worship and bow down: let us kneel before the Lord our maker.

For he is our God; and we are the people of his pasture, and the sheep of his hand.

Psalm 95:6,7a

Sing a new song to the Eternal, sing, all the earth, to the Eternal, sing to the Eternal, praise him, day after day tell of his saving aid.

Psalm 96:1,2
Moffatt's Trans.

You who love the Lord, hate evil! He preserves the souls of His saints; He delivers them out of the hand of the wicked.

Psalm 97:10 NKJV

Deliver us, O Lord our God, and gather us from among the nations, that we may give thanks to Your holy name and glory in praising You.

Psalm 106:47 AMP

Then they cried unto the Lord in their
trouble, and he delivered them out of
their distresses.

And he led them forth by the right
way.

Psalm 107:6,7a

Then they cried out to the Lord in their
trouble; He saved them out of their distresses.

He brought them out of darkness
and the shadow of death, and broke
their bands apart.

Psalm 107:13,14 NASB

Then they cried out to the Lord in their
trouble; He saved them out of their distresses.

He sent His word and healed them,
and delivered them from their destruc-
tions.

Psalm 107:19,20 NASB

Be thou exalted, O God, above the heavens: and thy glory above all the earth;

That thy beloved may be delivered: save with thy right hand, and answer me.

Psalm 108:5,6

Give us help from trouble: for vain is the help of man.

Through God we shall do valiantly: for he it is that shall tread down our enemies.

Psalm 108:12,13

Surely he shall not be moved for ever: the righteous shall be in everlasting remembrance.

He shall not be afraid of evil tidings: his heart is fixed, trusting in the Lord.

His heart is established, he shall not be afraid, until he see his desire upon his enemies.

Psalm 112:6-8

O Israel, trust the Lord! He is your helper. He is your shield.

O priests of Aaron, trust the Lord! He is your helper; he is your shield.

All of you, his people, trust in him.

He is your helper; he is your shield.

Jehovah is constantly thinking about us and he will surely bless us. He will bless the people of Israel and the priests of Aaron, and all, both great and small, who reverence him.

Psalm 115:9-13 TLB

From my distress I called upon the Lord; the Lord answered me and set me in a large place.

The Lord is for me; I will not fear; what can man do to me?

The Lord is for me among those who help me; therefore I shall look with satisfaction on those who hate me.

It is better to take refuge in the Lord than to trust in man.

It is better to take refuge in the Lord than to trust in princes.

All nations surrounded me; in the name of the Lord I will surely cut them off.

They surrounded me, yes, they surrounded me; in the name of the Lord I will surely cut them off.

They surrounded me like bees; they were extinguished as a fire of thorns; in the name of the Lord I will surely cut them off.

You pushed me violently so that I was falling, but the Lord helped me.

The Lord is my strength and song, and He has become my salvation.

The sound of joyful shouting and salvation is in the tents of the righteous; the right hand of the Lord does valiantly.

The right hand of the Lord is exalted; the right hand of the Lord does valiantly.

Psalm 118:5-16 NASB

You are my refuge and my shield; I have put my hope in your word.

Away from me, you evildoers, that I may keep the commands of my God!

Sustain me according to your promise, and I will live; do not let my hopes be dashed.

Uphold me, and I will be delivered; I will always have regard for your decrees.

Psalm 119:114-117 NIV

I will lift up mine eyes unto the hills, from whence cometh my help.

My help cometh from the Lord, which made heaven and earth.

He will not suffer thy foot to be

moved: he that keepeth thee will not slumber.

Behold, he that keepeth Israel shall neither slumber nor sleep.

The Lord is thy keeper: the Lord is thy shade upon thy right hand.

The sun shall not smite thee by day, nor the moon by night.

The Lord shall preserve thee from all evil: he shall preserve thy soul.

The Lord shall preserve thy going out and thy coming in from this time forth, and even for evermore.

Psalm 121:1-8

I lift mine eyes to the mountains; ah, where is help to come from?

Help comes from the Eternal who made heaven and earth.

Never will he let you slip; he who guards you never sleeps; he who guards Israel will neither sleep nor slumber.

The Eternal guards you, sheltering you upon the right; the sun shall never hurt you in the day, nor the moon by night.

The Eternal will guard you from all harm, he will preserve your life;

He will protect you as you come and

go, now and for evermore.

Psalm 121:1-8
Moffatt's Trans.

"If it had not been the Lord who was on our side," let Israel now say —

"If it had not been the Lord who was on our side, when men rose up against us.

Then they would have swallowed us alive, when their wrath was kindled against us;

Then the waters would have overwhelmed us, the stream would have gone over our soul;

Then the swollen waters would have gone over our soul."

Blessed be the Lord, who has not given us as prey to their teeth.

Our soul has escaped as a bird from the snare of the fowlers; the snare is broken, and we have escaped.

Our help is in the name of the Lord, who made heaven and earth.

Psalm 124:1-8 NKJV

They that trust in the Lord shall be as mount Zion which cannot be removed, but abideth for ever.

As the mountains are round about Jerusalem, so the Lord is round about his people from henceforth even for ever.

Psalm 125:1,2

Blessed is every one that feareth the Lord; that walketh in his ways.

For thou shalt eat the labour of thine hands: happy shalt thou be, and it shall be well with thee.

Psalm 128:1,2

But the Lord is righteous; he has cut me free from the cords of the wicked.

Psalm 129:4 NIV

I will clothe his enemies with shame, but the crown on his head will be resplendent.

Psalm 132:18 NIV

His foes I shroud with dark disgrace, but his own crown shall sparkle.

Psalm 132:18
Moffatt's Trans.

Though I walk in the midst of trouble, thou wilt revive me: thou shalt stretch forth thine hand against the wrath of mine enemies, and thy right hand shall save me.

Psalm 138:7

Deliver me, O Lord, from the evil man: preserve me from the violent man.

Keep me, O Lord, from the hands of the wicked; preserve me from the violent man; who have purposed to overthrow my goings.

O God the Lord, the strength of my salvation, thou hast covered my head in the day of battle.

Psalm 140:1,4,7

Surely the righteous shall give thanks unto thy name: the upright shall dwell in thy presence.

Psalm 140:13

Deliver me, O Lord, from mine enemies: I flee unto thee to hide me.

Teach me to do thy will; for thou art my God: thy spirit is good; lead me into the land of uprightness.

Quicken me, O Lord, for thy name's sake: for thy righteousness' sake bring my soul out of trouble.

And of thy mercy cut off mine enemies, and destroy all them that afflict my soul: for I am thy servant.

Psalm 143:9-12

Blessed be the Lord my strength, which teacheth my hands to war, and my fingers to fight:

My goodness, and my fortress; my high tower, and my deliverer; my shield, and he in whom I trust; who subdueth my people under me.

Psalm 144:1,2

Stretch forth Thy hand from on high; rescue me and deliver me out of great waters, out of the hand of aliens.

Psalm 144:7 NASB

The Lord upholdeth all that fall, and raiseth up all those that be bowed down.

Psalm 145:14

The Lord is near to all who call on him,

to all who call on him in truth.

He fulfills the desires of those who fear him; he hears their cry and saves them.

The Lord watches over all who love him, but all the wicked he will destroy.

Psalm 145:18-20 NIV

But whoso hearkeneth unto me shall dwell safely, and shall be quiet from fear of evil.

Proverbs 1:33

But safe he lives who listens to me; from fear of harm he shall be wholly free.

Proverbs 1:33
Moffatt's Trans.

He stores up sound wisdom for the upright; He is a shield to those who walk in integrity,

Guarding the paths of justice, and He preserves the way of His godly ones.

Proverbs 2:7,8 NASB

Discretion will guard you, understanding will watch over you,

71

To deliver you from the way of evil, from the man who speaks perverse things;

From those who leave the paths of uprightness, to walk in the ways of darkness.

Proverbs 2:11-13 NASB

My son, let them not depart from your eyes — keep sound wisdom and discretion;

So they will be life to your soul and grace to your neck.

Then you will walk safely in your way, and your foot will not stumble.

When you lie down, you will not be afraid; yes, you will lie down and your sleep will be sweet.

Do not be afraid of sudden terror, nor of trouble from the wicked when it comes;

For the Lord will be your confidence, and will keep your foot from being caught.

Proverbs 3:21-26 NKJV

Forsake her [wisdom] not, and she shall preserve thee: love her, and she shall keep thee.

Proverbs 4:6

72

The righteous will never be uprooted, but the wicked will not remain in the land.

Proverbs 10:30 NIV

Good men will never be displaced, but the wicked have no footing in the land.

Proverbs 10:30
Moffatt's Trans.

The integrity of the upright shall guide them.

Proverbs 11:3a

The righteous is delivered out of trouble, and the wicked cometh in his stead.

Proverbs 11:8

There shall no evil happen to the just: but the wicked shall be filled with mischief.

Proverbs 12:21

He that keepeth his mouth keepeth his life: but he that openeth wide his lips shall have destruction.

Proverbs 13:3

The lips of the wise shall preserve them.

Proverbs 14:3b

In the fear of the Lord is strong confidence: and his children shall have a place of refuge.

The fear of the Lord is a fountain of life, to depart from the snares of death.

Proverbs 14:26,27

Reverence for God gives a man deep strength; his children have a place of refuge and security.

Reverence for the Lord is a fountain of life; its waters keep a man from death.

Proverbs 14:26,27 TLB

He who ignores discipline despises himself, but whoever heeds correction gains understanding.

Proverbs 15:32 NIV

Pride goeth before destruction, and an haughty spirit before a fall.

Better it is to be of an humble spirit with the lowly, than to divide the spoil with the proud.

Proverbs 16:18,19

A fool's lips bring him strife, and his mouth invites a beating.

Proverbs 18:6 NIV

The name of the Lord is a strong tower: the righteous runneth into it, and is safe.

Proverbs 18:10

Do not say, "I will recompense evil"; wait for the Lord, and He will save you.

Proverbs 20:22 NKJV

Man's goings are of the Lord; how can a man then understand his own way?

Proverbs 20:24

Chargers are harnessed for the battle, but saving victory comes from the Eternal.

Proverbs 21:31
Moffatt's Trans.

There is no [human] wisdom or under-standing or counsel [that can prevail] against the Lord.

The horse is prepared for the day of battle, but deliverance and victory are of the Lord.

Proverbs 21:30,31 AMP

The fear of man bringeth a snare: but whoso putteth his trust in the Lord shall be safe.

Proverbs 29:25

Every word of God is pure: he is a shield unto them that put their trust in him.

Proverbs 30:5

Then the Lord will create above every dwelling place of Mount Zion, and above her assemblies, a cloud and smoke by day and the shining of a flaming fire by night. For over all the glory there will be a covering.

And there will be a tabernacle for shade in the daytime from the heat, for a place of refuge, and for a shelter from storm and rain.

Isaiah 4:5,6 NKJV

For thou hast been a strength to the poor, a strength to the needy in his distress, a refuge from the storm, a shadow from the heat, when the blast of the terrible ones is as a storm against the wall.

Isaiah 25:4

And thine ears shall hear a word behind thee, saying, This is the way, walk ye in it, when ye turn to the right hand, and when ye turn to the left.

Isaiah 30:21

And when you swerve to right or left, you hear a Voice behind you whispering, "This is the way, walk here."

Isaiah 30:21
Moffatt's Trans.

Woe to those who go down to Egypt for help, who rely on horses, who trust in the multitude of their chariots and in the great strength of their horsemen, but do not look to the Holy One of Israel, or seek help from the Lord.

Yet he too is wise and can bring disaster; he does not take back his words. He will rise up against the house of the wicked, against those who help evildoers.

But the Egyptians are men and not God; their horses are flesh and not spirit. When the Lord stretches out his hand, he who helps will stumble, he who is helped will fall; both will perish together.

This is what the Lord says to me: "As a lion growls, a great lion over his prey — and though a whole band of shepherds is called together against him, he is not frightened by their shouts or disturbed by their clamor — so the Lord Almighty will come down to do battle on Mount Zion and on its heights.

Like birds hovering overhead, the Lord Almighty will shield Jerusalem; he will shield it and deliver it, he will 'pass over' it and will rescue it."

Isaiah 31:1-5 NIV

And my people shall dwell in a peaceable habitation, and in sure dwellings, and in quiet resting places.

Isaiah 32:18

O Lord, be gracious unto us; we have waited for thee: be thou their arm every morning, our salvation also in the time of trouble.

Isaiah 33:2

But to us, O Lord, be merciful, for we have waited for you. Be our strength each day and our salvation in the time of trouble.

Isaiah 33:2 TLB

For the Lord is our judge, the Lord is our lawgiver, the Lord is our king; he will save us.

Isaiah 33:22

The Eternal himself rules us, the Eternal is our captain, the Eternal is our king, he, he alone, defends us.

*Isaiah 33:22
Moffatt's Trans.*

Strengthen ye the weak hands, and confirm the feeble knees.

Say to them that are of a fearful heart, Be strong, fear not: behold, your God will come with vengeance, even God with a recompence; he will come and save you.

Isaiah 35:3,4

Now therefore, O Lord our God, save us from his hand, that all the kingdoms of the earth may know that thou art the Lord, even thou only.

Isaiah 37:20

By the way that he came, by the same shall he return, and shall not come into this city, saith the Lord.

For I will defend this city to save it for mine own sake, and for my servant David's sake.

Isaiah 37:34,35

Behold, the Lord God will come with strong hand, and his arm shall rule for him: behold, his reward is with him, and his work before him.

He shall feed his flock like a shepherd: he shall gather the lambs with his arm, and carry them in his bosom, and shall gently lead those that are with young.

Isaiah 40:10,11

Fear not, for I am with you. Do not be dismayed. I am your God. I will strengthen you; I will help you; I will uphold you with my victorious right hand.

See, all your angry enemies lie confused and shattered. Anyone opposing you will die.

You will look for them in vain — they will all be gone.

I am holding you by your right hand — I, the Lord your God — and I say to you, Don't be afraid; I am here to help you.

Isaiah 41:10-13 TLB

Fear not [there is nothing to fear], for I am with you; do not look around you in terror and be dismayed, for I am your God. I will strengthen and harden you to difficulties, yes, I will help you; yes, I will hold you up and retain you with My [victorious] right hand of rightness and justice.

Behold, all they who are enraged and inflamed against you shall be put to shame and confounded; they who strive against you shall be as nothing and shall perish.

You shall seek those who contend with you but shall not find them; they who war against you shall be as nothing, as nothing at all.

For I the Lord your God hold your right hand; I am the Lord, Who says to you, Fear not; I will help you.

Isaiah 41:10-13 AMP

And I will bring the blind by a way that they knew not; I will lead them in paths that they have not known: I will make darkness light before them, and crooked things straight. These things will I do unto them, and not forsake them.

Isaiah 42:16

But now [in spite of past judgments for Israel's sins], thus says the Lord, He Who created you, O Jacob, and He Who formed you, O Israel: Fear not, for I have redeemed you [ransomed you by paying a price instead of leaving you captives]; I have called you by your name; you are Mine.

When you pass through the waters, I will be with you, and through the rivers, they will not overwhelm you. When you walk through the fire, you will not be burned or scorched, nor will the flame kindle upon you.

Isaiah 43:1,2 AMP

Fear not, for I redeem you, I claim you, you are mine.

I will be with you when you pass through waters, no rivers shall overflow you; when you pass through fire, you shall not be scorched, no flames shall burn you.

Isaiah 43:1b,2
Moffatt's Trans.

Do not fear, nor be afraid; have I not told you from that time, and declared it? You are My witnesses. Is there a God besides Me? Indeed there is no other Rock; I know not one.

Isaiah 44:8 NKJV

This is what the Lord says — your Redeemer, the Holy One of Israel: "I am the Lord your God, who teaches you what is best for you, who directs you in the way you should go."

Isaiah 48:17 NIV

This is what the Lord says: "In the time of my favor I will answer you, and in the day of salvation I will help you; I will keep you and will make you to be a covenant for the people, to restore the land and to reassign its desolate inheritances,

To say to the captives, 'Come out,' and to those in darkness, 'Be free!'

They will feed beside the roads and find pasture on every barren hill.

They will neither hunger nor thirst, nor will the desert heat or the sun beat upon them. He who has compassion on them will guide them and lead them beside springs of water."

Isaiah 49:8-10 NIV

I, even I, am he who comforts you. Who are you that you fear mortal men, the sons of men, who are but grass?

Isaiah 51:12 NIV

I have put my words in your mouth and covered you with the shadow of my hand — I who set the heavens in place, who laid the foundations of the earth, and who say to Zion, "You are my people."

Isaiah 51:16 NIV

The Lord has bared His holy arm in the sight of all the nations, that all the ends of the earth may see the salvation of our God.

Isaiah 52:10 NASB

"Though the mountains be shaken and the hills be removed, yet my unfailing love for you will not be shaken nor my covenant of peace be removed," says the Lord, who has compassion on you.

Isaiah 54:10 NIV

In righteousness you will be established: tyranny will be far from you; you will have nothing to fear. Terror will be far removed; it will not come near you.

If anyone does attack you, it will not be my doing; whoever attacks you will surrender to you.

Isaiah 54:14,15 NIV

"No weapon forged against you will

prevail, and you will refute every tongue that accuses you. This is the heritage of the servants of the Lord, and this is their vindication from me," declares the Lord.

Isaiah 54:17 NIV

No weapon forged against you shall succeed, no tongue raised against you shall win its plea. Such is the lot of the Eternal's servants; thus, the Eternal promises, do I maintain their cause.

Isaiah 54:17
Moffatt's Trans.

For thus saith the high and lofty One that inhabiteth eternity, whose name is Holy; I dwell in the high and holy place, with him also that is of a contrite and humble spirit, to revive the spirit of the humble, and to revive the heart of the contrite ones.

Isaiah 57:15

The Lord will guide you always; he will satisfy your needs in a sun-scorched land and will strengthen your frame. You will be like a well-watered garden, like a spring whose waters never fail.

Isaiah 58:11 NIV

Behold, the Lord's hand is not short-ened, that it cannot save; neither his ear heavy, that it cannot hear.

Isaiah 59:1

He put on might as armour, and victory as a helmet, and vengeance as his cloth-ing, and zeal to be his mantle.

In strict requital he repays his foes with fury and his enemies with shame, till in the far west men have awe of the Eternal, and in the east they see his bril-liant deeds; for his vengeance pours out like a pent-up stream, driven by a blast of wind, but to Sion he comes for deliv-erance, to free Jacob from its rebels.

As for me, the Eternal declares, this is my compact with them: "My spirit which rests upon you, and the words I have put into your lips, shall never depart from your lips, nor from the lips of your descendants, nor from the lips of their descendants," the Eternal declares, "from henceforth and for ever."

Isaiah 59:17-21
Moffatt's Trans.

He put on righteousness as armor, and the helmet of salvation on his head. He clothed himself with robes of vengeance and of godly fury.

He will repay his enemies for their evil deeds — fury for his foes in distant-lands.

Then at last they will reverence and glorify the name of God from west to east. For he will come like a flood-tide driven by Jehovah's breath.

He will come as a Redeemer to those in Zion who have turned away from sin.

"As for me, this is my promise to them," says the Lord: "My Holy Spirit shall not leave them, and they shall want the good and hate the wrong — they and their children and their children's children forever."

Isaiah 59:17-21 TLB

And I will make thee unto this people a fenced brasen wall: and they shall fight against thee, but they shall not prevail against thee: for I am with thee to save thee and to deliver thee, saith the Lord.

And I will deliver thee out of the hand of the wicked, and I will redeem thee out of the hand of the terrible.

Jeremiah 15:20,21

Blessed is the man that trusteth in the Lord, and whose hope the Lord is.

For he shall be as a tree planted by the waters, and that spreadeth out her roots by the river, and shall not see when heat cometh, but her leaf shall be green; and shall not be careful in the year of drought, neither shall cease from yielding fruit.

Jeremiah 17:7,8

But the Lord is with me as a mighty terrible one: therefore my persecutors shall stumble, and they shall not prevail: they shall be greatly ashamed; for they shall not prosper: their everlasting confusion shall never be forgotten.

Jeremiah 20:11

But the Lord is with me like a mighty warrior; so my persecutors will stumble and not prevail. They will fail and be thoroughly disgraced; their dishonor will never be forgotten.

Jeremiah 20:11 NIV

"But I will gather the remnant of My flock out of all countries where I have driven them, and bring them back to their folds; and they shall be fruitful and increase.

"I will set up shepherds over them who will feed them; and they shall fear no more, nor be dismayed, nor shall they be lacking," says the Lord.

Jeremiah 23:3,4 NKJV

"So do not fear, O Jacob my servant; do not be dismayed, O Israel," declares the Lord. "I will surely save you out of a distant place, your descendants from the land of their exile. Jacob will again have peace and security, and no one will make him afraid."

Jeremiah 30:10 NIV

But I will deliver thee in that day, saith the Lord: and thou shalt not be given into the hand of the men of whom thou art afraid.

For I will surely deliver thee, and thou shalt not fall by the sword, but thy life shall be for a prey unto thee: because thou hast put thy trust in me, saith the Lord.

Jeremiah 39:17,18

Be not afraid of the king of Babylon, of whom ye are afraid; be not afraid of him, saith the Lord: for I am with you to save you, and to deliver you from his hand.

And I will shew mercies unto you, that he may have mercy upon you, and cause you to return to your own land.

Jeremiah 42:11,12

And they shall dwell safely therein, and shall build houses, and plant vineyards; yea, they shall dwell with confidence, when I have executed judgments upon all those that despise them round about them; and they shall know that I am the Lord their God.

Ezekiel 28:26

For this is what the Sovereign Lord says: I myself will search for my sheep and look after them.

As a shepherd looks after his scattered flock when he is with them, so will

I look after my sheep. I will rescue them from all the places where they were scattered on a day of clouds and darkness.

I will bring them out from the nations and gather them from the countries, and I will bring them into their own land. I will pasture them on the mountains of Israel, in the ravines and in all the settlements in the land.

I will tend them in a good pasture, and the mountain heights of Israel will be their grazing land. There they will lie down in good grazing land, and there they will feed in a rich pasture on the mountains of Israel.

I myself will tend my sheep and have them lie down, declares the Sovereign Lord.

I will search for the lost and bring back the strays. I will bind up the injured and strengthen the weak, but the sleek and the strong I will destroy. I will shepherd the flock with justice."

Ezekiel 34:11-16 NIV

Then King Nebuchadnezzar was astonished; and he rose in haste and spoke, saying to his counselors, "Did we not cast three men bound into the midst of the fire?" They answered and said to the king, "True, O king."

"Look!" he answered, "I see four men loose, walking in the midst of the fire; and they are not hurt, and the form of the fourth is like the Son of God."

Then Nebuchadnezzar went near the mouth of the burning fiery furnace and spoke, saying, "Shadrach, Meshach, and Abed-Nego, servants of the Most High God, come out, and come here." Then Shadrach, Meshach, and Abed-Nego came from the midst of the fire.

And the satraps, administrators, governors, and the king's counselors gathered together, and they saw these men on whose bodies the fire had no power; the hair of their head was not singed nor were their garments affected, and the smell of fire was not on them.

Nebuchadnezzar spoke, saying, "Blessed be the God of Shadrach, Meshach, and Abed-Nego, who sent His Angel and delivered His servants who trusted in Him, and they have frustrated the king's word, and yielded their bodies, that they should not serve nor worship any god except their own God!

"Therefore I make a decree that any

people, nation, or language which speaks anything amiss against the God of Shadrach, Meshach, and Abed-Nego shall be cut in pieces, and their houses shall be made an ash heap; because there is no other God who can deliver like this."

Daniel 3:24-29 NKJV

So the king gave the order, and they brought Daniel and threw him into the lions' den. The king said to Daniel, "May your God, whom you serve continually, rescue you!"

A stone was brought and placed over the mouth of the den, and the king sealed it with his own signet ring and with the rings of his nobles, so that Daniel's situation might not be changed. Then the king returned to his palace and spent the night without eating and without any entertainment being brought to him. And he could not sleep.

At the first light of dawn, the king got up and hurried to the lions' den. When he came near the den, he called to Daniel in an anguished voice, "Daniel, servant of the living God, has your God, whom·you serve continually, been able to rescue you from the lions?"

Daniel answered, "O king, live forever! My God sent his angel, and he shut the mouths of the lions. They have not hurt me, because I was found innocent in his sight. Nor have I ever done any wrong before you, O king."

The king was overjoyed and gave orders to lift Daniel out of the den. And when Daniel was lifted from the den, no wound was found on him, because he had trusted in his God.

Daniel 6:16-23 NIV

O man greatly beloved, fear not: peace be unto thee be strong, yea, be strong. And when he had spoken unto me, I was strengthened, and said, Let my lord speak; for thou hast strengthened me.

Daniel 10:19

But I will have mercy upon the house of Judah, and will save them by the Lord their God, and will not save them by bow, nor by sword, nor by battle, by horses, nor by horsemen.

Hosea 1:7

And in that day will I make a covenant for them with the beasts of the field, and with the fowls of heaven, and with the creeping things of the ground: and I will break the bow and the sword and the battle out of the earth, and will make them to lie down safely.

Hosea 2:18

And by a prophet the Lord brought Israel out of Egypt, and by a prophet was he preserved.

Hosea 12:13

And it shall come to pass, that whosoever shall call on the name of the Lord shall be delivered: for in mount Zion and in Jerusalem shall be deliverance, as the Lord hath said, and in the remnant whom the Lord shall call.

Joel 2:32

Therefore I will look unto the Lord; I will wait for the God of my salvation: my God will hear me.

Rejoice not against me, O mine enemy: when I fall, I shall arise; when I sit in darkness, the Lord shall be a light unto me.

Micah 7:7,8

The Lord is good, a strong hold in the day of trouble; and he knoweth them that trust in him.

Nahum 1:7

Whatever they plot against the Lord he will bring to an end; trouble will not come a second time.

Nahum 1:9 NIV

"The Lord your God is with you, he is mighty to save. He will take great delight in you, he will quiet you with his love, he will rejoice over you with singing."

"The sorrows for the appointed feasts I will remove from you; they are a burden and a reproach to you.

"At that time I will deal with all who oppressed you; I will rescue the lame and gather those who have been scattered. I will give them praise and honor in every land where they were put to shame."

"At that time I will gather you; at that time I will bring you home. I will give you honor and praise among all the peoples of the earth when I restore your fortunes before your very eyes," says the Lord."

Zephaniah 3:17-20 NIV

I lifted up mine eyes again, and looked, and behold a man with a measuring line in his hand.

Then said I, Whither goest thou? And he said unto me, To measure Jerusalem, to see what is the breadth thereof, and what is the length thereof.

And, behold, the angel that talked with me went forth, and another angel went out to meet him,

And said unto him, Run, speak to this young man, saying, Jerusalem shall be inhabited as towns without walls for the multitude of men and cattle therein:

For I, saith the Lord, will be unto her a wall of fire round about, and will be the glory in the midst of her.

Zechariah 2:1-5

So will I save you, and ye shall be a blessing: fear not, but let your hands be strong.

Zechariah 8:13b

Turn you to the strong hold, ye prisoners of hope: even to day do I declare that I will render double unto thee.

Zechariah 9:12

The Lord of hosts will defend them; they shall devour and subdue with slingstones. They shall drink and roar as if with wine; they shall be filled with blood like basins, like the corners of the altar.

The Lord their God will save them in that day, as the flock of His people. For they shall be like the jewels of a crown, lifted like a banner over His land.

Zechariah 9:15,16 NKJV

And I will rebuke the devourer for your sakes, and he shall not destroy the fruits of your ground; neither shall your vine cast her fruit before the time in the field, saith the Lord of hosts.

Malachi 3:11

Now the birth of Jesus Christ was on this wise: When as his mother Mary was espoused to Joseph, before they came together, she was found with child of the

Holy Ghost.

Then Joseph her husband, being a just man, and not willing to make her a publick example, was minded to put her away privily.

But while he thought on these things, behold, *the angel of the Lord appeared unto him in a dream*, saying, Joseph, thou son of David, fear not to take unto thee Mary thy wife: for that which is conceived in her is of the Holy Ghost.

And she shall bring forth a son, and thou shalt call his name JESUS: for he shall save his people from their sins.

Now all this was done, that it might be fulfilled which was spoken of the Lord by the prophet, saying,

Behold, a virgin shall be with child, and shall bring forth a son, and they shall call his name Emmanuel, which being interpreted is, God with us.

Then Joseph being raised from sleep did as the angel of the Lord had bidden him, and took unto him his wife:

And knew her not till she had brought forth her firstborn son: and he called his name JESUS.

Matthew 1:18-25

Then Herod, having called the learned men secretly, ascertained accurately from them the length of time since the star's appearance, and sending them to Bethlehem he said, Having proceeded on your way, conduct an exhaustive and accurate investigation concerning the child, and after you discover that for which you are seeking, bring back the news to me in order that I also, having come, may render homage to him. And having heard the king, they proceeded on their way.

And behold, the star which they saw in its rising kept on going before them until, having come, it stood above where the young child was. And having seen the star, they rejoiced with great joy, exceedingly. And having come into the house, they saw the young child with Mary, His mother, and having fallen down, they prostrated themselves in homage before Him. And having opened their treasure-chests, they brought to Him gifts, gold, and frankincense, and myrrh. *And having been warned in a dream not to return to Herod, by another road they went back to their country.*

Now, after they had returned, behold, *an angel of the Lord appears in a dream to Joseph,* saying, Having arisen, take at once under your care the young child and His mother and be fleeing into Egypt, and be there until I tell you. For Herod is about to be seeking the young child to destroy Him. And having arisen, he took the young child and His mother under his care by night and withdrew to Egypt.

And he was there until the death of Herod, in order that there might be fulfilled that which was spoken by the Lord through the prophet, saying, Out of Egypt I called my Son.

Matthew 2:7-15
The Wuest New Testament

But Herod having died, behold, *an angel of the Lord appeared in a dream to Joseph in Egypt,* saying, Having arisen, take the young child and His mother under your care and be proceeding into the land of Israel, for those who seek the life of the young child have died.

And having arisen, he took the young child and His mother under his care and went to the land of Israel. However, having heard that Archelaus was reigning as king in Judaea instead of his father, Herod, he was afraid to go there. *And having been warned in a dream,* he withdrew into the regions of Galilee. And having come, he established his home in a city called Nazareth, in order that there might be fulfilled that which was spoken through the prophets, A Nazarene shall He be called.

Matthew 2:19-23
The Wuest New Testament

Remember, I am sending you out as my Messengers like sheep among wolves. So be as wise as serpents, and as blameless as doves. Be on your guard against your fellow men, for they will betray you to courts of law, and scourge you in their Synagogues; and you will be brought before governors and kings for my sake, that you may witness for me before them and the nations.

Whenever they betray you, do not be anxious as to how you shall speak or what you shall say, for what you shall say will be given you at the moment; for it will not be you who speak, but the Spirit of your Father that speaks within you.

Brother will betray brother to death, and the father his child; and children will turn against their parents, and cause them to be put to death; and you will be hated by every one on account of my Name. Yet the man that endures to the end shall be saved. But, when they persecute you in one town, escape to the next; for, I tell you, you will not have come to the end of the towns of Israel before the Son of Man comes.

A scholar is not above his teacher, nor a servant above his master. It is enough for a scholar to be treated like his teacher, and a servant like his master. If the head of the house has been called Baal-zebub, how much more the members of his household! Do not, therefore, be afraid of them. There is nothing concealed which will not be revealed, nor anything hidden which will not become known.

What I tell you in the dark, say again in the light; and what is whispered in your ear, proclaim upon the house-tops. And do not be afraid of those who kill the body, but are unable to kill the soul; rather be afraid of him who is able to destroy both soul and body in Hell.

Are not two sparrows sold for a penny? Yet not one of them will fall to the ground without your Father's knowledge. While as for you, the very hairs of your head are all numbered. Do not, therefore, be afraid; you are of more value than many sparrows.

Matthew 10:16-31
The Twentieth Century
New Testament

But the angel spoke to the women, "Do not be afraid. I know that you are looking for Jesus who was crucified. He is not here — he has been raised, just as he said.

"Come and look at the place where he was lying. Then go quickly and tell his disciples that he has been raised from the dead. And, listen, he goes before you into Galilee; you will see him there! Now I have told you my message."

Then the women went away quickly from the tomb, their hearts filled with awe and great joy, and ran to give the news to his disciples. But quite suddenly, Jesus stood before them in their path, and said, "Peace be with you!" and they went forward to meet him, and clasping his feet, worshipped him. Then Jesus said to them, "Do not be afraid. Go and tell my brothers to go off now into Galilee and they shall see me there."

Matthew 28:5-10
J. B. Phillips Trans.

And all who heard it kept it in mind, asking one another — "What can this child be destined to become?" For the Power of the Lord was with him.

Then his father Zechariah was filled with the Holy Spirit, and, speaking under inspiration, said:

"Blessed is the Lord, the God of Israel, Who has visited his people and wrought their deliverance,

"And has raised up for us the Strength of our Salvation in the House of his servant David —

"As he promised by the lips of his holy Prophets of old — Salvation from our enemies and from the hands of all that hate us,

"Showing mercy to our forefathers, and mindful of his sacred Covenant.

"This was the oath which he swore to our forefather Abraham — That we should be rescued from the hands of our enemies,

"And should serve him without fear in holiness and righteousness, in his presence all our days.

"And thou, Child, shalt be called Prophet of the Most High, for thou shalt go before the Lord to make ready his way,

"To give to his people the knowledge of salvation in the forgiveness of their sins,

"Through the tender mercy of our God, whereby the Dawn will break on us from Heaven,

"To give light to those who dwell in darkness and the shadow of death, and guide our feet into the Way of Peace."

> *Luke 1:66-79*
> *The Twentieth Century*
> *New Testament*

Do not be afraid, little flock, for your Father has been pleased to give you the kingdom.

> *Luke 12:32 NIV*

Whosoever shall seek to save his life shall lose it; and whosoever shall lose his life shall preserve it.

Luke 17:33

But there shall not an hair of your head perish.

Luke 21:18

And you shall know the truth, and the truth shall make you free.

Therefore if the Son makes you free, you shall be free indeed.

John 8:32,36 NKJV

Verily, verily, I say unto you, He that entereth not by the door into the sheep-fold, but climbeth up some other way, the same is a thief and a robber.

But he that entereth in by the door is the shepherd of the sheep.

To him the porter openeth; and the sheep hear his voice: and he calleth his own sheep by name, and leadeth them out.

And when he putteth forth his own sheep, he goeth before them, and the sheep follow him: for they know his voice.

And a stranger will they not follow, but will flee from him: for they know not the voice of strangers...

My sheep hear my voice, and I
know them, and they follow me.

John 10:1-5,27

My sheep listen to my voice; I know
them, and they follow me; and I give
them Immortal Life, and they shall not
be lost; nor shall anyone snatch them
out of my hands. What my Father has
entrusted to me is more than all else;
and no one can snatch anything out of
the Father's hands. The Father and I are
one.

John 10:27-30
The Twentieth Century
New Testament

Howbeit when he, the Spirit of truth, is
come, he will guide you into all truth:
for he shall not speak of himself; but
whatsoever he shall hear, that shall he
speak: and he will shew you things to
come.

John 16:13

These things I have spoken unto you,
that in me ye might have peace. In the

world ye shall have tribulation: but be of
good cheer; I have overcome the world.

John 16:33

I pray not that thou shouldest take them
out of the world, but that thou
shouldest keep them from the evil.

John 17:15

I do not ask that You will take them out
of the world, but that You will keep and
protect them from the evil one.

John 17:15 AMP

And when Herod was about to bring
him out, that night Peter was sleeping,
bound with two chains between two sol-
diers; and the guards before the door
were keeping the prison.

Now behold, an angel of the Lord
stood by him, and a light shone in the
prison; and he struck Peter on the side
and raised him up, saying, "Arise quickly!" And his chains fell off his hands.

Then the angel said to him, "Gird
yourself and tie on your sandals"; and so
he did. And he said to him, "Put on your
garment and follow me."

So he went out and followed him,

and did not know that what was done by the angel was real, but thought he was seeing a vision.

When they were past the first and the second guard posts, they came to the iron gate that leads to the city, which opened to them of its own accord; and they went out and went down one street, and immediately the angel departed from him.

And when Peter had come to himself, he said, "Now I know for certain that the Lord has sent His angel, and has delivered me from the hand of Herod and from all the expectation of the Jewish people."

Acts 12:6-11 NKJV

Then spake the Lord to Paul in the night by a vision, Be not afraid, but speak, and hold not thy peace:

For I am with thee, and no man shall set on thee to hurt thee: for I have much people in this city.

Acts 18:9,10

For there stood by me this night the

angel of God, whose I am, and whom I serve,

Saying, Fear not, Paul; thou must be brought before Caesar: and, lo, God hath given thee all them that sail with thee.

Wherefore, sirs, be of good cheer: for I believe God, that it shall be even as it was told me.

Acts 27:23-25

For there took a stand at my side this night a messenger of the God whose I am and to whom I render sacred service, saying, Stop fearing, Paul. It is necessary in the nature of the case for you to stand before Caesar.

And behold, God has graciously safeguarded for you all those who are sailing with you. On which account be having courage, men, for I trust God that it shall be in the manner as it has been told me.

Acts 27:23-25
The Wuest New Testament

Much more, therefore, being now justified by His blood, shall we be saved from the wrath of God through Him.

For if, while we were enemies, we were reconciled to God through the death of His Son; much more, having been reconciled, shall we be saved by His life;

And not only so, but we are rejoicing in God through our Lord Jesus Christ, through Whom we now received the reconciliation.

For, if, by the trespass of the one, death reigned through the one; much more shall those who receive the abundance of the grace, and of the gift of righteousness, reign in life through the One, Jesus Christ.

Romans 5:9-11,17
The Worrell New Testament

Consequently, there is now no condemnation to those who are in Christ Jesus.

For the law of the Spirit of life in Christ Jesus made me free from the law of sin and death.

Romans 8:1,2
The Worrell New Testament

If God be for us, who can be against us?

Romans 8:31b

Yet amid all these things we more than conquer through him who loved us!

Romans 8:37
The Twentieth Century
New Testament

Yet amid all these things we are more than conquerors and gain a surpassing victory through Him Who loved us.

Romans 8:37 AMP

The Lord Jesus, on the night he was betrayed, took bread, and when he had given thanks, he broke it and said, "This is my body, which is for you; do this in remembrance of me." In the same way, after supper he took the cup, saying, "This cup is the new covenant in my blood; do this, whenever you drink it, in remembrance of me." For whenever you eat this bread and drink this cup, you proclaim the Lord's death until he comes.

Therefore, whoever eats the bread or drinks the cup of the Lord in an unworthy manner will be guilty of sinning against the body and blood of the

Lord. A man ought to examine himself before he eats of the bread and drinks of the cup. For anyone who eats and drinks without recognizing the body of the Lord eats and drinks judgment on himself. That is why many among you are weak and sick, and a number of you have fallen asleep. But if we judged ourselves, we would not come under judgment. When we are judged by the Lord, we are being disciplined so that we will not be condemned with the world.

1 Corinthians 11:23b-32 NIV

So that there should be no division in the body, but that its parts should have equal concern for each other. If one part suffers, every part suffers with it; if one part is honored, every part rejoices with it.

Now you are the body of Christ, and each one of you is a part of it. And in the church God has appointed first of all apostles, second prophets, third teachers, then workers of miracles, also those having gifts of healing, those able to help others, those with gifts of administration, and those speaking in different kinds of tongues.

1 Corinthians 12:25-28 NIV

Finally, be strong in the Lord, and in the strength of His might.

Put on the full armor of God, that you may be able to stand firm against the schemes of the devil.

For our struggle is not against flesh and blood, but against the rulers, against the powers, against the world forces of this darkness, against the spiritual forces of wickedness in the heavenly places.

Therefore, take up the full armor of God, that you may be able to resist in the evil day, and having done everything, to stand firm.

Stand firm therefore, having girded your loins with truth, and having put on the breastplate of righteousness,

And having shod your feet with the preparation of the gospel of peace;

In addition to all, taking up the shield of faith with which you will be able to extinguish all the flaming missiles of the evil one.

And take the helmet of salvation, and the sword of the Spirit, which is the word of God.

With all prayer and petition pray at all times in the Spirit, and with this in view, be on the alert with all perseverance and petition for all the saints.

Ephesians 6:10-18 NASB

And in nothing terrified by your adversaries: which is to them an evident token of perdition, but to you of salvation, and that of God.

Philippians 1:28

But what things were gain to me, these I accounted loss for Christ.

Nay, more, I even account all things to be loss for the excellency of the knowledge of Christ Jesus my Lord, for whose sake I suffered the loss of all things, and account them refuse, that I may gain Christ.

Philippians 3:7,8
The Worrell New Testament

Who hath delivered us from the power of darkness, and hath translated us into the kingdom of his dear Son.

Colossians 1:13

So then, just as you received Christ Jesus as Lord, continue to live in him, rooted and built up in him, strengthened in the faith as you were taught, and overflowing with thankfulness.

Colossians 2:6,7 NIV

See that no one render to any one evil for evil; but always pursue that which is good, toward one another, and toward all.

Rejoice always; pray without ceasing. In everything give thanks; for this is God's will in Christ Jesus respecting you.

Quench not the Spirit. Despise not prophesyings; but prove all things, hold fast that which is good. Abstain from every form of evil.

And the God of peace Himself sanctify you wholly; and may your spirit and soul and body be preserved entire, without blame at the coming of our Lord Jesus Christ.

1 Thessalonians 5:15-23
The Worrell New Testament

Therefore, brethren, stand fast, and hold the traditions which ye have been taught, whether by word, or our epistle.

Now our Lord Jesus Christ himself, and God, even our Father, which hath loved us, and hath given us everlasting consolation and good hope through grace,

Comfort your hearts, and stablish you in every good word and work.

2 Thessalonians 2:15-17

But the Lord is faithful, who shall stablish you, and keep you from evil.

2 Thessalonians 3:3

The Lord will draw me to himself away from every pernicious work actively opposed to that which is good, and will keep me safe and sound for His kingdom, the heavenly one, to whom be the glory forever and forever. Amen.

2 Timothy 4:18
The Wuest New Testament

Since then the children share in flesh and blood, He Himself likewise also partook of the same, that through death He might render powerless him who had the power of death, that is, the devil;

119

And might deliver those who through fear of death were subject to slavery all their lives.

For assuredly He does not give help to angels, but He gives help to the descendants of Abraham.

Therefore, He had to be made like His brethren in all things, that He might become a merciful and faithful high priest in things pertaining to God, to make propitiation for the sins of the people.

For since He Himself was tempted in that which He has suffered, He is able to come to the aid of those who are tempted.

Hebrews 2:14-18 NASB

God himself has said — "I will never forsake you, nor will I ever abandon you." Therefore we may say with confidence — "The Lord is my helper, I will not be afraid. What can man do to me?"

Hebrews 13:5b,6
The Twentieth Century
New Testament

Submit yourselves therefore to God.

Resist the devil, and he will flee from you.

James 4:7

For he who desires to be loving life and to see good days, let him stop the natural tendency of his tongue from evil, and the natural tendency of his lips to the end that they speak no craftiness, but let him rather at once and once for all turn away from evil and let him do good. Let him seek peace and pursue it, because the Lord's eyes are directed in a favorable attitude towards the righteous, and His ears are inclined unto their petitions, but the Lord's face is against those who practice evil things.

And who is he that will do you evil if you become zealots of the good? But if even you should perchance suffer for the sake of righteousness, you are spiritually prosperous ones. Moreover, do not be affected with fear of them by the fear which they strive to inspire in you, neither become agitated, but set apart Christ as Lord in your hearts, always being those who are ready to present a verbal defense to everyone who asks you for a logical explanation concerning the hope which is in all of you, but doing this with meekness and a wholesome serious caution, having a conscience unimpaired, in order that in the very thing in which they defame you, they may be put to shame, those who spitefully abuse, insult, and traduce your good behavior which is in Christ; for it is better when doing good, if perchance it be the will of God that you be suffering, rather than when doing evil.

1 Peter 3:10-17
The Wuest New Testament

Casting all your care upon him; for he careth for you.

1 Peter 5:7

Casting the whole of your care [all your anxieties, all your worries, all your concerns, once and for all] on Him, for He cares for you affectionately and cares about you watchfully.

1 Peter 5:7 AMP

But, if our lives are lived in the Light, as God himself is in the Light, we have communion with one another, and the Blood of Jesus, his Son, purifies us from all sin.

> *1 John 1:7*
> *The Twentieth Century*
> *New Testament*

To him who is able to keep you from falling and to present you before his glorious presence without fault and with great joy —
To the only God our Savior be glory, majesty, power and authority, through Jesus Christ our Lord, before all ages, now and forevermore! Amen.

> *Jude 24,25 NIV*

And then he placed his right hand upon me and said, "Do not be afraid. I am the first and the last, the living one. I am he who was dead, and now you see me alive for timeless ages!"

> *Revelation 1:17b,18*
> *J. B. PHILLIPS*

And they overcame him by the blood of the Lamb, and by the word of their testi-

their testimony; and they loved not their lives unto the death.

Revelation 12:11

References

Other Harrison House Spirit-Filled Pocket Bibles

The Spirit-Filled Pocket Bible on Faith
The Spirit-Filled Pocket Bible on Healing
The Spirit-Filled Pocket Bible on Finances

Available from your local bookstore

HARRISON HOUSE
Tulsa, Oklahoma 74153